NAMED AS ONE OF THE
TOP TEN
PLACES TO WORK
IN THE FEDERAL GOVERNMENT

National Transportation Safety Board
Information Technology
Strategic Plan
FY2010 – FY2015

A Key Component in Achieving NTSB's Mission

December 1, 2009

National
Transportation
Safety Board

Table of Contents

Information Technology will continue to become a more important *component* in support of the National Transportation Safety Board's Mission:

> *To promote transportation safety by*
> - *maintaining our congressionally mandated independence and objectivity;*
> - *conducting objective, precise accident investigations and safety studies;*
> - *performing fair and objective airman and mariner certification appeals; and*
> - *advocating and promoting safety recommendation; and*
>
> *to assist victims of transportation accidents and their families.*

Over the past three years the IT infrastructure of the Safety Board has been refreshed, major applications have been upgraded and replatformed, the IT security posture of the agency has been greatly improved and we have deployed information technologies to enhance the capture, transport management and sharing of information across the organization. However, we continue to seek opportunities for improving service to our customers while reducing costs.

This year, the Office of the Chief Information Officer continued its work to establish an effective foundation for improving the delivery of IT products and services at the National Transportation Safety Board (NTSB). One component of that foundation is the refinement of the IT Strategic Plan, to correspond with the release of a new Strategic Plan for the Safety Board.

I believe that an effective way to measure the performance of an IT organization, or any organization, is to apply maturity models. Ultimately, the success of an IT organization relies upon its people, its processes and its technology. As a result, I am fully committed to effectively utilizing process maturity models to achieve and measure results; enhancing IT Security to protect our systems against future vulnerabilities and threats; and preparing our IT workforce for future requirements. To achieve an IT organization that fully supports the Safety Board the Office of the Chief Information Officer has established seven IT Strategic Goals and corresponding Focus Areas: *Enterprise Architecture, IT Security, E-Government, IT Capital Planning & Investment Control (CPIC), IT Infrastructure, Information and Records Management, and IT Workforce Management*.

The employees in the Office of the Chief Information Officer have at least one item, if not multiple items that highlights their contribution to support the office and the Safety Board as a whole.

Executive Summary

The National Transportation Safety Board's Information Technology Strategic Plan provides a specific course of action for effectively managing the Information Technology (IT) Program in support of the Safety Board's overall Mission. NTSB's IT strategy guides IT resources to align with the business goals and establishes specific IT Strategic Goals with Focus Areas and performance measures. This document is our roadmap to achieve targeted results in providing reliable services, meeting customer expectations, and creating savings.

To meet the current and future needs of customers, stakeholders and employees, the Safety Board's exchange and management of information is based on strategic plans that will improve our capacity for delivering mission results. As a key component in achieving Safety Board's mission success, the IT structure is based on strategic plans that incorporate the concepts of electronic government and modern IT enterprise architecture.

The Safety Board's emerging governance framework will embrace the distinct modal needs and serves as the foundation for the Board's IT strategy. Our modal and support offices serve as leaders for a variety of NTSB initiatives, as well as recognized leaders in their specific fields of endeavor. The goal is to establish and mature an overall framework for integrating business needs and IT. This framework will facilitate cooperation and improve data sharing capabilities within and across modal lines and with the Safety Board's customers and stakeholders.

The Office of the Chief Information Officer has identified seven IT Strategic Goals to maximize the innovative and effective use of technology during the migration of its IT portfolio to integrated, agency-wide business processes and technologies.

NTSB IT Strategic Goals

Enterprise Architecture (EA): Leverage EA to improve NTSB's mission performance and realize its strategic goals and objectives.

IT Security: Protect the availability, confidentiality and integrity of NTSB's IT resources.

E-Government: Improve the efficiency and effectiveness of NTSB business processes.

IT Capital Planning & Investment Control (CPIC): Improve the planning, execution and management of IT investments.

IT Infrastructure: Provide enterprise solutions – improving the quality, accessibility, and information sharing capabilities between NTSB and its customers.

Information and Records Management: Create an effective knowledge-sharing environment while meeting information management standards and requirements.

IT Workforce Management: Ensure the availability of IT human capital capable of meeting the goals and NTSB mission challenges.

Our strategy establishes the usage of process maturity models including those of the Government Accountability Office (GAO), Office of Management and Budget (OMB), National Institute of Standards and Technology (NIST), and the Federal CIO Council. The long-term goals and performance measures maintain our focus on the bottom line – specific results that we must achieve to be successful in accomplishing our IT Mission.

Intensive efforts have been underway to standardize IT functions and organizations throughout the Federal Government. These efforts will continue to affect NTSB to varying degrees in the coming years. Further standardization along business lines will enable NTSB to accrue costs savings. When opportunities that make business sense arise, NTSB will move to take advantage of Lines of Business solutions.

The Office of the Chief Information Officer will continue to implement business and IT initiatives while upgrading information technologies, improving security, and bringing better connections to personnel in the field. We will establish policies that create consistent practices; and develop teams, tactics, and tools to cut cycle time, reduce friction, and improve communication. At the same time, we will work to spread best business practices across the Safety Board. These collective approaches will improve performance, reduce inefficiency and duplication, and provide the support needed to achieve our Mission.

Section 1: Introduction

This section introduces key factors that influenced the formation of the Safety Board's
IT Strategic Plan.

Purpose

The National Transportation Safety Board is embarking on a more structured, goal and
results oriented planning process both from a strategic and operational planning
perspective. A component of this overall effort is the refinement of the IT Strategic Plan.
The Information Technology Strategic Plan builds upon and aligns with the National
Transportation Safety Board's FY2010 – FY2015 Strategic Plan. The IT Strategic Plan
serves as a catalyst to implement agency-wide business process and technology
improvements designed to strengthen the Safety Board's success in delivering Mission
results.

Scope

This IT Strategic Plan provides a specific course of action for integrating the Safety Board's
IT strategic planning process with the Board's Strategic Plan for Fiscal Years 2010 through
2015.

The IT Strategic Plan supports the Safety Board's strategic mission and management
goals and aligns IT with the Safety Board's major program concerns. The IT Strategic
Goals are aligned with seven specific focus areas; *Enterprise Architecture, IT Security,
E-Government, IT Capital Planning & Investment Control (CPIC), IT Infrastructure,
Information and Records Management, and IT Workforce Management.*

IT Challenges

There are many challenges that the Safety Board will continue to encounter including
new IT mandates, funding, and limited human resources. Simultaneously, there are
rising challenges for enhanced security and safety in support of Homeland Security
initiatives; rapid changes in technology; retirement of the "baby boomer" generations and
its impact to the IT Workforce; as well as increased expectations of stakeholders for
innovative and faster IT service applications.

The Safety Board recognizes that making smart investments, integrating architectures,
ensuring secure IT environments, and providing an adequate IT workforce are vital to
overcoming these challenges and fulfilling its Strategic Plan. The Safety Board must
leverage IT resources through enterprise solutions and increased partnerships, in fulfilling
its ultimate commitment of improving IT performance and guaranteeing efficient and
effective customer-oriented business operations.

Legislation and Presidential Directives

The Safety Board recognizes the need to adapt to changes mandated by the Administration and Congress and has developed an IT strategy to address legislation and presidential orders that include, but are not limited to, the items identified below. *Note: Legislation and Presidential Directives are accessible via http://www.whitehouse.gov/omb/.*

- FY 2002 President's Management Agenda (PMA)
- E-Government Act of 2002
- Federal Information Security Management Act (FISMA) of 2002
- OMB's Federal Enterprise Architecture Program
- IT Management Reform Act of 1996 (ITMRA) or Clinger-Cohen Act
- Federal Acquisition Reform Act of 1996 (FARA)
- Government Paperwork Elimination Act 1998 (GPEA)
- Government Management Reform Act of 1994 (GMRA)
- Federal Acquisition Streamlining Act of 1994 (FASA)
- Paperwork Reduction Act of 1995 (PRA)
- Presidential Decision Directive 63 (PDD-63)
- Government Performance and Results Act of 1993 (GPRA)
- Chief Financial Officers Act of 1990 (CFO Act)
- Privacy Act of 1974
- The Freedom of Information Act (FOIA)
- The Federal Records Act (FRA)
- Federal Financial Management Improvement Act (FFMFIA)
- Section 508, Rehabilitation Act of 1998 (29 U.S.C. 794d)
- Rehabilitation Act Amendments (Section 508)
- OMB Circulars:
  - A-11 Preparation, Submission and Execution of the Budget
  - A-130: Management of Federal Information Resources
  - A-16: Coordination of Geographic Information and Related Spatial Data Activities
  - A-76: "Performance of Commercial Activities"
- Homeland Security Presidential Directive (HSPD-12)
- Openness Promotes Effectiveness in our National Government Act of 2007
- Open Government Directive (OMB M-10-06)

Section 2: Strategic Framework

This section presents an overview of the high level linkages between the National Transportation Safety Board's FY 2010 – 2015 Strategic Plan and the Board's IT Strategic Plan FY 2010 – 2015

The Office of the Chief Information Officer seven IT Strategic Goals, presented earlier in this document, have distinct and specific mappings to the National Transportation Safety Board's FY 2010 – 2015 Strategic Plan. An overview of the mappings are presented below and an overview of NTSB' Strategic Plan Framework is presented on the following page for a more detailed frame of reference.

NTSB IT Strategic Goals

Enterprise Architecture (EA): Leverage EA to improve NTSB's mission performance and realize its strategic goals and objectives. *(maps to NTSB Strategic Goal #3 – Outstanding Stewardship of Resources and Strategic Goal #4 – Organizational Excellence)*

IT Security: Protect the availability, confidentiality and integrity of NTSB's IT resources. *(maps to NTSB Strategic Goal #3 – Outstanding Stewardship of Resources)*

E-Government: Improve the efficiency and effectiveness of NTSB business processes. *(maps to NTSB Strategic Goal #1 – Accomplish Objective Investigations of Transportation Accidents, Strategic Goal# 2 – From Investigations, Recommend and Advocate Actions that will Improve Transportation Safety and Strategic Goal #3 – Outstanding Stewardship of Resources)*

IT Capital Planning & Investment Control (CPIC): Improve the planning, execution and management of IT investments. *(maps to NTSB Strategic Goal #3 – Outstanding Stewardship of Resources)*

IT Infrastructure: Provide enterprise solutions—improving the quality, accessibility, and information sharing capabilities between NTSB and its customers. *(maps to NTSB Strategic Goal #3 – Outstanding Stewardship of Resources)*

Information and Records Management: Create an effective knowledge-sharing environment while meeting information management standards and requirements. *(maps to NTSB Strategic Goal #3 – Outstanding Stewardship of Resources and Strategic Goal #4 – Organizational Excellence)*

IT Workforce Management: Ensure the availability of IT human capital capable of meeting the goals and NTSB mission challenges. (maps to NTSB Strategic Goal #4 – Organizational Excellence)

NTSB Strategic Plan 2010 - 2015 Framework

NTSB Mission

The NTSB's mission is to promote transportation safety by

- maintaining our congressionally mandated independence and objectivity;
- conducting objective, precise accident investigations and safety studi
- performing fair and objective airman and mariner certification appeals; and
- advocating and promoting safety recommendations, and

to assist victims of transportation accidents and their families.

Vision	Values	Strategic Goals
We identify and promote lessons learned from accident investigations to help make transportation safer.	The NTSB embraces the values of integrity, objectivity, and thoroughness in our work. We are committed to these values every day and in every way.	<ul><li>Accomplish objective investigations of transportation accidents.</li><li>From investigations, recommend and advocate actions that will improve transportation safety</li><li>Outstanding stewardship of resources</li><li>Organizational excellence</li></ul>

Key Business Principles:
Plan Execute Measure

Investigations

Strategic Goal - Accomplish Objective Investigations of Transportation Accidents

Strategic Objectives:

- Make Judicious Selections of Accidents to Investigate in Each Transportation Mode,
- Appropriately Scale the Investigative Response to Accidents, and
- Develop and Maintain State-of-the-Art Investigative and Procedural Tools for Accident Investigations

Impact on Safety

Strategic Goal - From Investigations, Recommend and Advocate Actions that will Improve Transportation Safety

Strategic Objectives:

- Provide Objective and Independent Advice on Transportation Safety Issues,
- Engage in Outreach with the Transportation Community to Advance Safety,
- Advocate the Implementation of Safety Recommendations with Emphasis on the Most Wanted List of Transportation Safety Improvements
- Constructively Affect the Transportation Industry, and
- Maintain a Fair and Expeditious Appeals Process for Airmen and Mariners

Stewardship

Strategic Goal - Outstanding Stewardship of Resources

Strategic Objectives:

- Employ Project Management Best Practices to Maximize the Effective Use of Agency Resources while Maintaining High Quality,
- Effectively Use the Allocated Funds to Execute the Mission, and
- Utilize Effective Information Technology to Accomplish the Organization's Mission

Excellence

Strategic Goal - Organizational Excellence

Strategic Objectives:

- Integrate Long-Range Planning in All Elements of NTSB Business,
- Align and Improve Human Capital Planning,
- Maintain a Competent and Effective Workforce through Targeted Training and Employee Development,
- Foster Effective Internal Communications, and
- Improve Investigative Readiness by Identifying Emerging Safety Issues

NTSB IT Strategic Plan FY 2010 - 2015: IT Mission, Vision, and IT Strategic Principles

<u>*IT Mission*</u>: *To enable the execution of the NTSB safety mission by providing information technology services that support and improve key work processes.*

<u>*IT Vision*</u>: *The vision of the Office of the Chief Information Officer is to apply a best practice, integrated approach to providing technology products and services in support of NTSB's mission and customers.*

IT Strategic Principles

The following Strategic Principles provide the framework for delivering our IT Mission

- *Alignment: The Safety Board's* strategic mission and management goals will be supported by aligning IT with major program areas.

- *Enterprise Approach:* To maximize effective use of technology, the Safety Board will migrate to integrated, agency-wide business processes and technologies.

- *Teamwork:* Offices will serve as partners for a variety of IT initiatives. This approach fosters shared ownership, embraces diversity, leverages strengths and is consistent with best practices.

- *Process Maturity:* Continuous improvement in IT processes will be achieved by following appropriate process maturity models.

- *Measurable:* Achievement of strategic goals will be measurable and reported regularly.

- *Support for Best Practices:* IT strategic goals will address legislative, regulatory and administrative mandates such as FISMA, OMB A-130, HSPD-12, etc.

Goal 1:
Enterprise Architecture
Leverage EA to improve NTSB's mission performance and realize its strategic goals and objectives

Goal 7:
Workforce Management
Ensure the availability of IT human capital capable of meeting the goals and NTSB mission challenges

Goal 2:
IT Security
Protect the availability, confidentiality, and integrity of NTSB's IT resources

NTSB IT Strategic Goals
Directly Support NTSB Strategic Goals:

1 - Accomplish Objective Investigations of Transportation Accidents

2 - From Investigations, Recommend and Advocate Actions that will Improve Transportation Safety

3 - Outstanding Stewardship of Resources, and

4 - Organization Excellence

Goal 6:
Information & Records Management
Create an effective knowledge sharing environment, safeguarding records, privacy, and accessibility

Goal 3:
E-Government
Improve the efficiency and effectiveness of NTSB business processes

Goal 5:
IT Infrastructure
Provide enterprise operation - improving the quality, accessibility, and sharing of data between NTSB and its customers

Goal 4:
IT Capital Planning
Improve the planning, execution, and management of IT investments

See APPENDIX – A SELECTED OUTCOME AND SUPPORTING ACTIVITY MEASURES FOR SELECTED OUTCOME AND ACTIVITY MEASURES THAT SUMMARIZE OCIO SUPPORT FOR THE SAFETY BOARD'S FOUR STRATEGIC GOALS.

The Safety Board's IT Strategic Goals directly link to the goals indicated in *OMB's A-130 Maturity Assessment Tracking* guide to provide more effective management for the achievement of the vision. The diagram below illustrates how these goals map to process areas defined by OMB Circular A-130.

Process Maturity Models

Progress in achieving IT Strategic Goals will be measured using a process maturity model that is specific to meeting the requirements of that goal. The Capability Maturity Model Integration (CMMI) illustrated below describes an evolutionary improvement path from an ad-hoc, immature process to a mature, disciplined process. A comparable model will be used to define specific goals and to measure progress for each IT Strategic Goal. Maturity Models used in this plan are based upon industry, international or federal government models widely used in the IT community.

Capability Maturity Model (CMMI) *

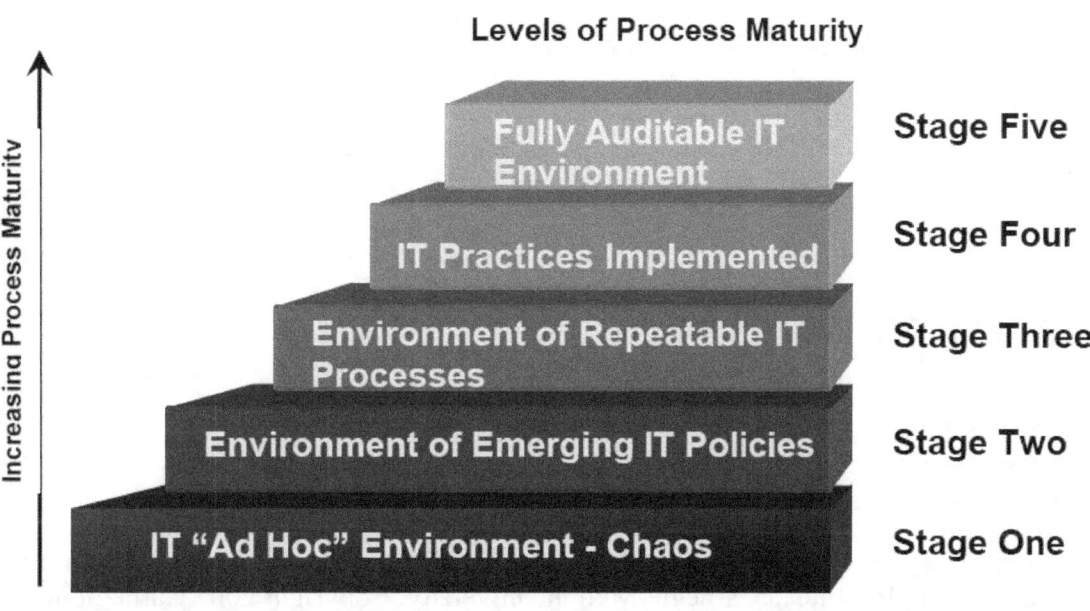

Levels of Process Maturity

Fully Auditable IT Environment	Stage Five
IT Practices Implemented	Stage Four
Environment of Repeatable IT Processes	Stage Three
Environment of Emerging IT Policies	Stage Two
IT "Ad Hoc" Environment - Chaos	Stage One

Increasing Process Maturity

* The Capability Maturity Model (CMMI®) was developed by the Software Engineering Institute at Carnegie-Mellon University.

Process, People, Technology

In the Capability Maturity Model Integration (CMMI) Version 1.2* Overview (http://www.sei.cmu.edu/library/assets/cmmi-overview071.pdf) the integrated role of Process, People and Technology is highlighted. From the perspective of CMMI:

"While process is often described as a node on the process-people-technology triad, it can also be considered the "glue" that ties the triad together. Everyone realizes the importance of having a motivated, quality work force but even our finest people cannot perform at their best when the process is not understood or operating at its best. Process, people and technology are the major determinants of product cost, schedule, and quality."

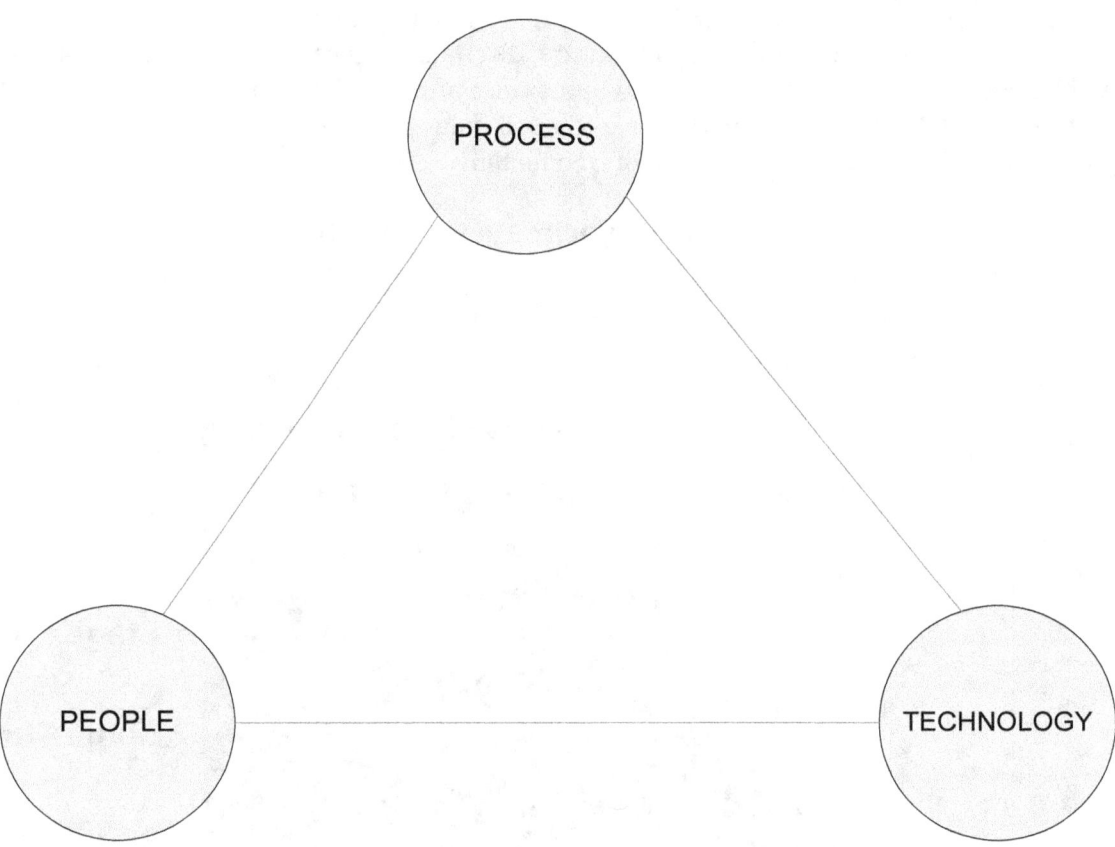

* Capability Maturity Model Integration (CMMI®) was developed by the Software Engineering Institute at Carnegie-Mellon University. Copyright 2007 Carnegie-Mellon University

Section 4: IT Strategic Goals and Focus Areas

To more effectively manage the achievement of the IT Vision, an IT Strategic Focus Area has been directly aligned with each IT Strategic Goal. Focus Areas provide key information, the Long Term Strategic Goal, the Process Maturity Model to Measure progress, and Objectives.

Focus Area 1: Enterprise Architecture (EA)

Enterprise Architecture (EA) continues to mature as a discipline at the National Transportation Safety Board. As is the case with this plan, the goal is to not reinvent the wheel but rather draw upon best practices developed across the Government in the EA arena. The goal of the EA Program is to ensure IT aligns with the Safety Board's major program concerns.   IT alignment will be achieved through an iterative process of mapping business processes, reducing/eliminating redundancies, and through the development of transition plans that will drive the continual refresh and upgrade of infrastructure and applications to meet current and emerging mission needs. Through this iterative process, the EA Program will also contribute to the effective alignment of the underlying IT investment portfolio.

Long Term Strategic Goal

The goal of Enterprise Architecture (EA) is to improve the Safety Board's mission performance and realize its strategic goals and objectives. EA seeks to achieve this goal by:

- Providing strategic business and architecture consulting services to program areas
- Improving the connection between stakeholders and investments
- Streamlining the processes and business rules in the program areas
- Minimizing system redundancies
- Improving data integration and data sharing
- Increasing the re-use of IT assets
- Reducing the total cost of ownership of the Safety Board's IT Portfolio

To carry out the iterative EA process and establish a transition the Enterprise Architect will follow a modified version of the Department of Interior's Methodology for Business Transformation (MBT). The methodology identifies opportunities for improving mission performance and internal efficiencies and allows for the development of a transition plan for implementing these opportunities for improvement.

Methodology for Business Transformation (MBT)

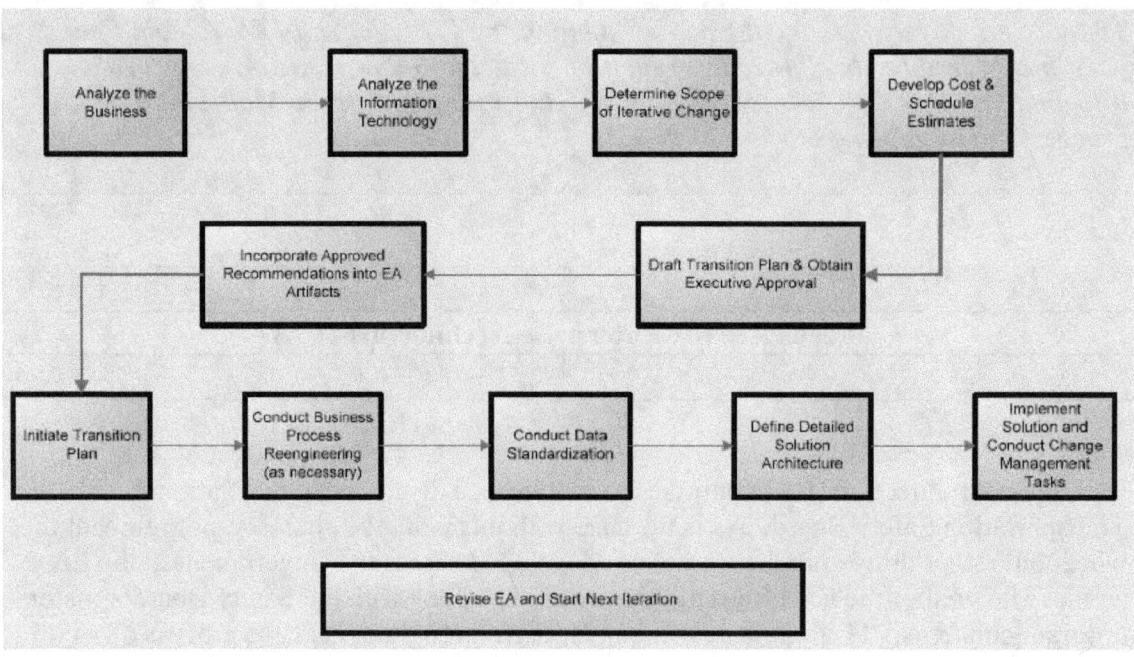

Process Maturity Model/Performance Measure

During the first years of this plan, the Safety Board will continue to use **OMB's Enterprise Architecture (EA) Maturity Framework v2.0** to measure the agency's progress in this strategic goal.

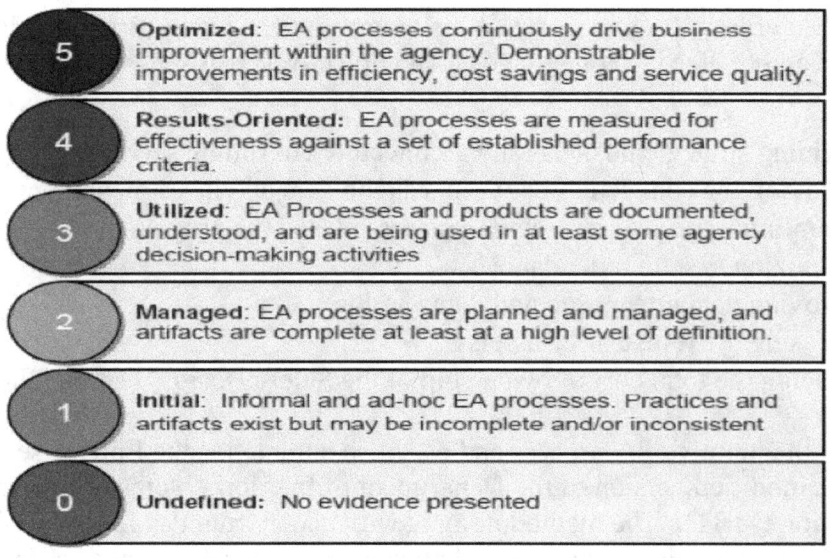

The Safety Board will also transition to **OMB's Enterprise Architecture Assessment Framework v3.1** during the life of this plan and has worked to fully integrate EA into Capital Planning and Investment Control (CPIC) and System Development Life Cycle (SDLC) processes at the NTSB.

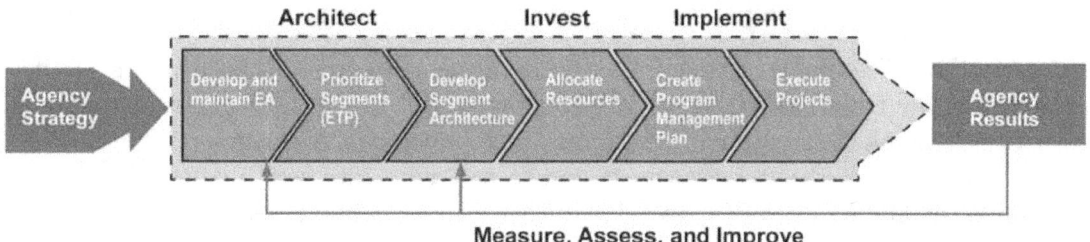

Information and IT-Enabled Performance Improvement Lifecycle

FY10 – FY15 Objectives

- Complete Business Process Modeling
- Complete initial DRM model
- Retire redundant systems identified in Transition Plans
- Adhere to emerging Federal EA Principles
- Facilitate NTSB submissions to Data.gov
- Self Assess and Measure Progress Against the OMB EA Maturity Framework *(annual)*
- All EA models will be kept current and compliant with the FEA *(annual)*
- Initiate the development of new Transition Plans based on prioritization actions *(annual)*
- Release updated versions of the five EA Models as appropriate *(annual)*

Stretch Objective(s)

- No current stretch objective(s) for this focus area.

Focus Area 2: IT Security

The Safety Board is committed to continuing improvements in its IT security program, and to complying with OMB Circular A-130, Appendix III Security Requirements. The Safety Board maintains a number of systems to support modal and support office mission. This complexity makes security and IT management a very challenging undertaking, and underscores the need for further standardization.

Long Term Strategic Goal

The goal of Information Security is to protect the availability, confidentiality and integrity of the Safety Board's information technology resources. This goal is achieved through the application of requirements specified in OMB Circular A-130, the Federal Information Security Management Act (FISMA) and various U.S. Commerce Department's National Institute of Standards and Technology (NIST) publications. The NTSB IT Security Program uses a risk-based, cost-effective approach to secure information and systems, identify and resolve current IT security weaknesses and risks, and protect against future vulnerabilities and threats.

As shown in the table below, NIST has defined 17 areas that must be addressed as part of an excellent Information Security program. These 17 elements must be addressed in order to achieve the long-term strategic goal for this focus area.

NIST Security Program Elements

1. Risk Management
2. Review of Security Controls
3. Life Cycle
4. Authorize Processing (Certification & Accreditation)
5. System Security Plan
6. Personnel Security
7. Physical and Environmental Protection
8. Production, Input/Output Controls
9. Contingency Planning
10. Hardware and System Software Maintenance
11. Data Integrity
12. Documentation
13. Security Awareness, Training, and Education
14. Incident Response Capability
15. Identification and Authentication
16. Logical Access Controls
17. Audit Trails

The Certification & Accreditation (C&A) process is a key component of the security program as it consolidates many of the 17 program elements on a system-by-system basis. The Safety Board has adopted an iterative process to reach a level of maturity consistent with resources available.

The process is depicted below:

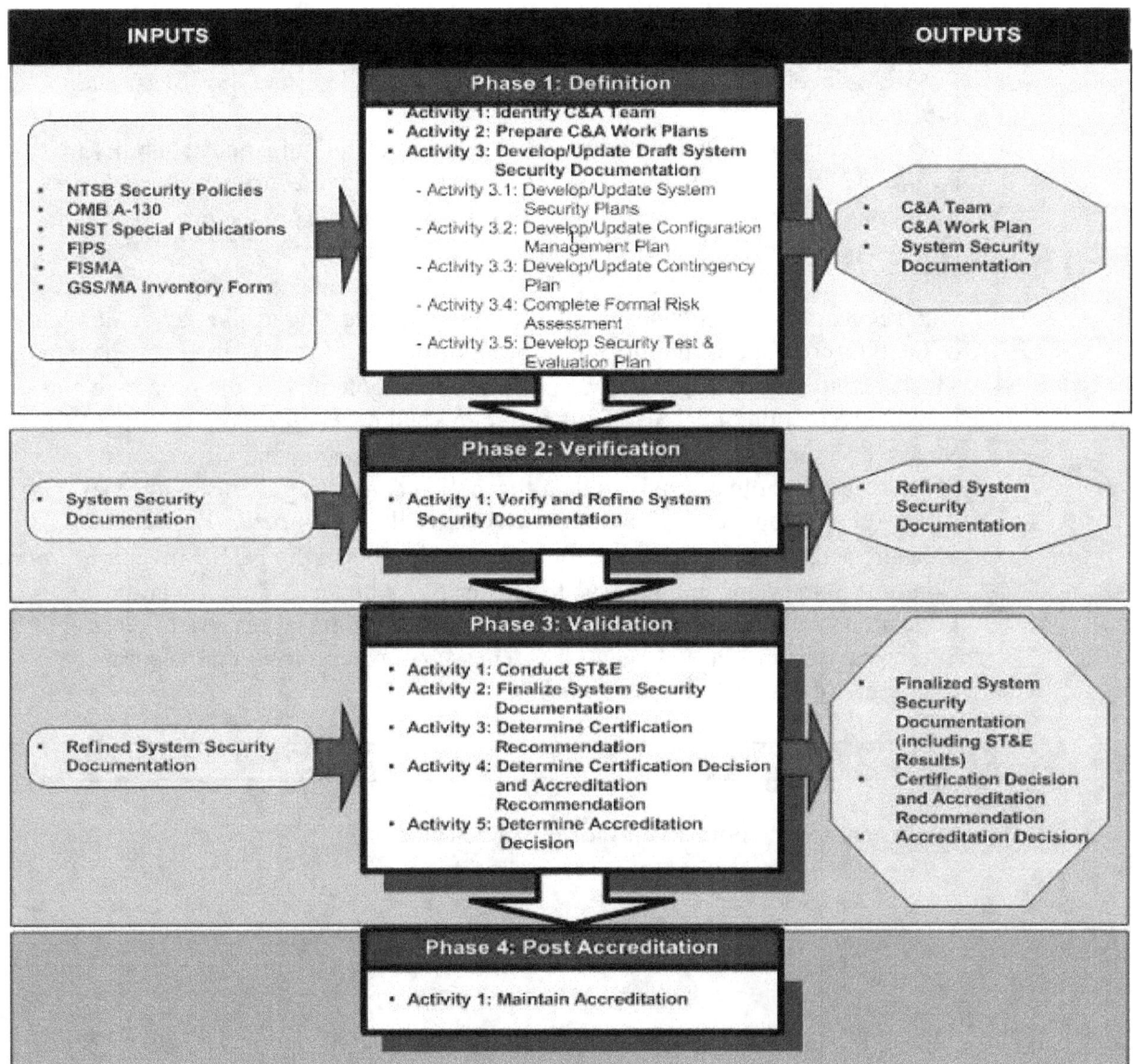

Process Maturity Model/Performance Measure

The Annual FISMA Report Process will be used to measure NTSB's progress in this strategic focus area.

- C&A remaining system in the NTSB inventory
- Maintain a continuous program assessing the security controls within NTSB maintained information systems by following NIST Special Publication 800-53A
- Modify NTSB IT Security program in accordance with guidance provided by NIST Special Publication 800-37 Revision 1 *Guide for Applying the Risk Management Framework to Federal Information Systems* as applicable.
- POA&M development and execution for any items identified in FISMA audit *(annual)*
- Mature and improve the existing policy, procedure and guidance capability to ensure the foundation of the NTSB IT security program *(annual)*
- Mature and improve Incident Response Capability to ensure the proactive and reactive protection of NTSB infrastructure and data *(annual)*
- Measure and improve the existing risk management and compliance programs with regular vulnerability scanning and penetration testing as the key components of OCIO's continuous monitoring efforts *(annual)*
- Measure and improve Incident Response Capability to ensure the proactive and reactive protection of NTSB IT infrastructure and data *(annual)*
- Measure and improve security controls and procedures for the protection of privacy data and other sensitive data for mobile computing devices, internal databases and applications, and remote access solutions *(annual)*
- Measure and maintain C&A for 100% of the systems in the NTSB inventory *(annual)*
- Continue to measure and improve the Security Awareness, Training and Education Program to ensure at least 95% of NTSB employees, contractors and interns have an increased level of awareness and experience commensurate to their areas of responsibility *(annual)*

Stretch Objective(s)

- No current stretch objective(s) for this focus area.

E-Government has distinct and different meanings to individuals and organizations. For the purposes of this plan, E-Government refers to the use of technology to deliver improvements in the Safety Board's mission areas and the Safety Board's partnership with existing and emerging Government-wide technology initiatives. For example, NTSB currently partners with the Department of the Interior for financial and other services as part of their participation in the Human Resources and the Financial Management Lines of Business offerings.

E-Government Initiatives

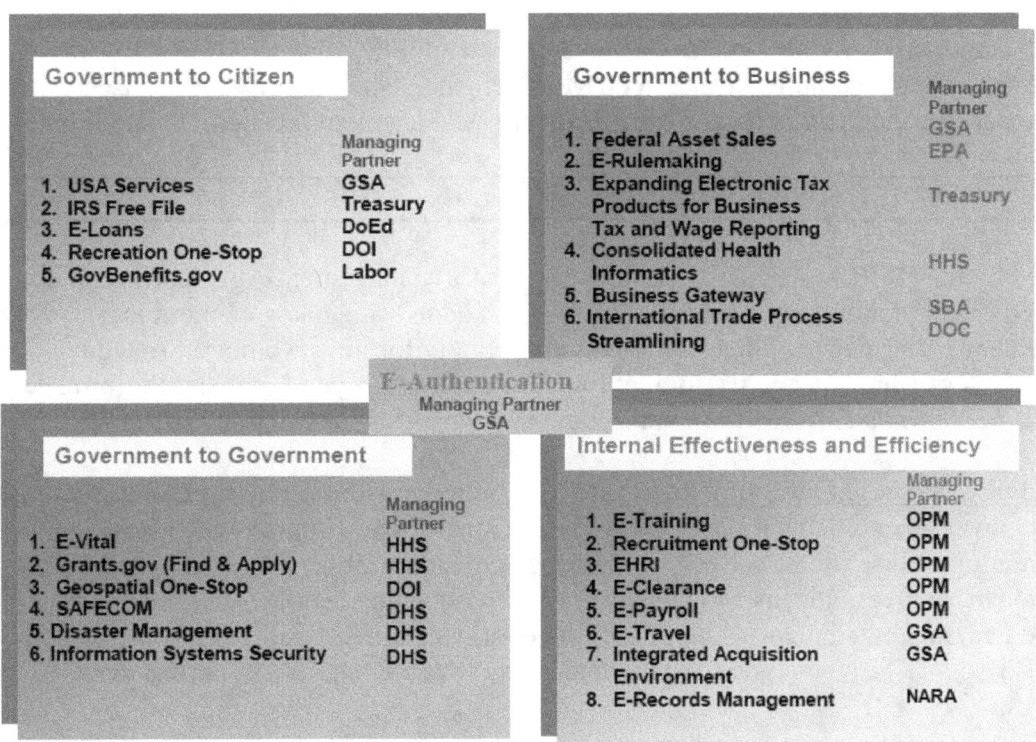

E-Government initiatives cut across multiple Federal agencies and address opportunities to provide services in the areas of Government to Citizen, Government to Business, Government to Government and Internal Effectiveness. Current initiatives in each of these areas are summarized in the diagram above.

Long Term Strategic Goal

The goal of E-Government is to improve the efficiency and effectiveness of the Safety Board's business processes. E-Government technology will enable us to do our jobs better. Using Safety Board's emerging Enterprise Architecture program the Office of the Chief Information Officer will explore and map NTSB mission needs and continue to look for opportunities for E-Government investment.

Another facet of the Safety Board's Strategic Goal regarding E-Government will include the development of a strong Project Management practice. The Safety Board will use Project Management throughout OCIO, and recognizes that the scope and nature of the Board's efforts undertaken as part of E-Gov will require strong PM skills. As a result, individuals in the System Support and Enterprise Architecture Divisions will serve as mentors for Project Management in OCIO.

This goal is directly supported by several of the other goals identified in this plan, in the EA, IT Security and IT Infrastructure focus areas. In addition, this focus area covers the areas of Section 508 compliance and Web Management. The maturity model used to measure performance in this area is the President's Management Agenda.

The President's Management Agenda (PMA)

Released by the OMB in August 2001, the President's Management Agenda (PMA) identified five mutually reinforcing initiatives, each addressing a key element in management performance with a significant opportunity for improvement: Strategic Management of Human Capital; Competitive Sourcing; Improved Financial Performance; *Expanded Electronic Government*, and Budget and Performance Integration.

Expanded Electronic Government: This PMA initiative launched to make better use of Federal Government information technology (IT) investments, improve the accessibility of information and services, and reduce response time to citizens. The vision for e-Government involves citizens and businesses easily obtaining services and interacting with the Federal Government while improving overall efficiency and effectiveness. The Safety Board's IT Strategic goals are aligned with PMA e-Government performance measures.

Process Maturity Model/Performance Measure

This aggressive strategy focuses on managing areas of weakness across the government, and making improvements where the most progress can be achieved. OMB measures and scores each Federal agency's PMA performance on a quarterly basis with its *Stoplight Scoring System*. The PMA Scorecard employs a simple grading system common today in well-run businesses: Green for success, Yellow for mixed results, and Red for unsatisfactory. One of the factors included in the scorecard is the Enterprise Architecture maturity score discussed in Focus Area 1. Additional scorecard items applicable to this focus area include IT Security, Privacy and Project Management.

Open Government Initiative

Released by the OMB in December 2009, the Open Government Directive instructs every government agency to take immediate, specific steps to open their doors and data to the American People. The three core principles of transparency, participation, and collaboration form the cornerstone of an open government:

- **Transparency.** Government should provide citizens with information about what their government is doing so that government can be held accountable.
- **Participation.** Government should actively solicit expertise from outside Washington so that it makes policies with the benefit of the best information.
- **Collaboration.** Government officials should work together with one another and with citizens as part of doing their job of solving national problems.

FY10 –FY 15 Objectives

- Deploy agency-wide Project Tracking System
- Enhance NTSB application functionality
- Enhance Safety Board's use of regulations.gov and other e-gov/center of excellence solutions
- Participate in the development of the NTSB Open Government Plan
- Facilitate and support transparency improvements
- Develop, maintain, and facilitate a sound and integrated web-related information technology architecture for the Safety Board by improving the quality of the Intranet and Internet web sites
- 90% of E-Gov projects within 10% of the goals established in the cost, schedule, and performance baseline *(FY11)*
- 95% of E-Gov projects within 10% of the goals established in the cost, schedule, and performance baseline *(FY12)*
- Achieve PMP certification for at least 75% of Systems Support Division staff *(FY13)*
- Assess NTSB production systems per Steady State CPIC Phase requirements *(annual)*
- Partner with Enterprise Architect on development and execution of Transition Plan *(annual)*
- Review NTSB web sites for compliance with applicable Federal statutes and directives *(annual)*

Stretch Objective(s)

- Implement a customizable portal to allow Safety Board employees to have access to job specific applications on their "desktop" *(FY10)*

Long Term Strategic Goal

The goal of Capital Planning is to improve the planning, execution and management of
IT investments. The overall process for Capital Planning varies slightly from
organization to organization but should include the five sequential phases represented in
the diagram below.

NTSB Capital Planning and Investment Control (CPIC) Process

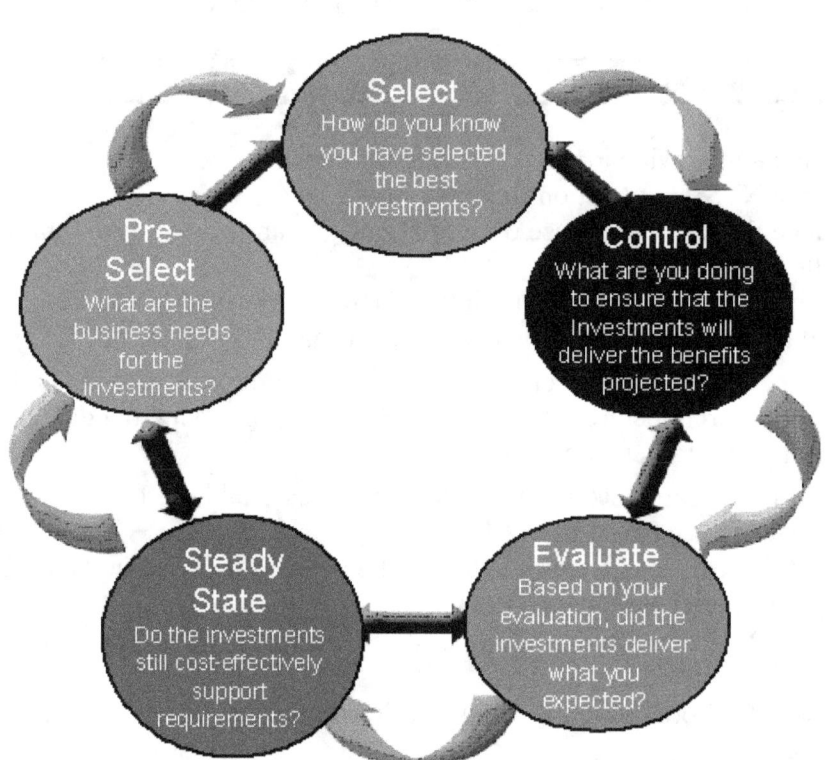

Activities supporting the Capital Planning Focus Area are integrated to activities in the
Enterprise Architecture Focus Area. Capital Planning defines a process for reviewing,
approving and monitoring investments. Enterprise Architecture ensures that the
investments being made are not redundant and that they support mission goals.

The goal over the next few years is to introduce standard CPIC processes to the Safety
Board on a scale that is consistent with the threshold of IT investment dollars. These

changes will be consistent with best practices and consistent with the GAO IT Investment Management (ITIM) Framework.

Investment Review Board (IRB): IT Portfolio Decision-Making

NTSB IT Investment Review Board (IRB): Collaborative IT Governance process

IT investments at the Safety Board are effectively managed but through processes that are outside standard CPIC processes. As the Safety Board progresses through the FY2010 – FY2015 Strategic Planning cycle the Board expects the IT Investment process to mature considerably. One of the steps in the CPIC process is to establish an IRB that makes "smarter" recommendations on the viability and prioritization of proposed initiatives; prevent duplicate investments; and leverage shared solutions, where appropriate. The IRB will ensure the NTSB IT Portfolio follows Management Objectives and Business Priorities criteria as listed.

Management Objectives - Criteria to evaluate investments in the CPIC Process.
- Implement legal and judicial mandates
- Respond to internal and executive mandates
- Obtain positive return on investments
- Improve performance (showing links to NTSB Strategic Plan and performance goals, avoiding duplication, managing risk, improving efficiency, achieving specific objectives)

Business Priorities - The second tier of management guidance for portfolio decisions
- Enterprise projects
- Projects on schedule, within costs, meeting expectations (evaluated through control reviews)
- Projects that are consistent with EA Transition Plan
- Management objectives and business priorities provide general guidance.

Process Maturity Model

Progress in the Capital Planning focus area will be tracked using the GAO IT Investment Management (ITIM) Framework.

See next page for GAO IT Investment Management (ITIM) Framework.

GAO's Investment Technology Investment Management (ITIM) Model (GAO-04-394G)

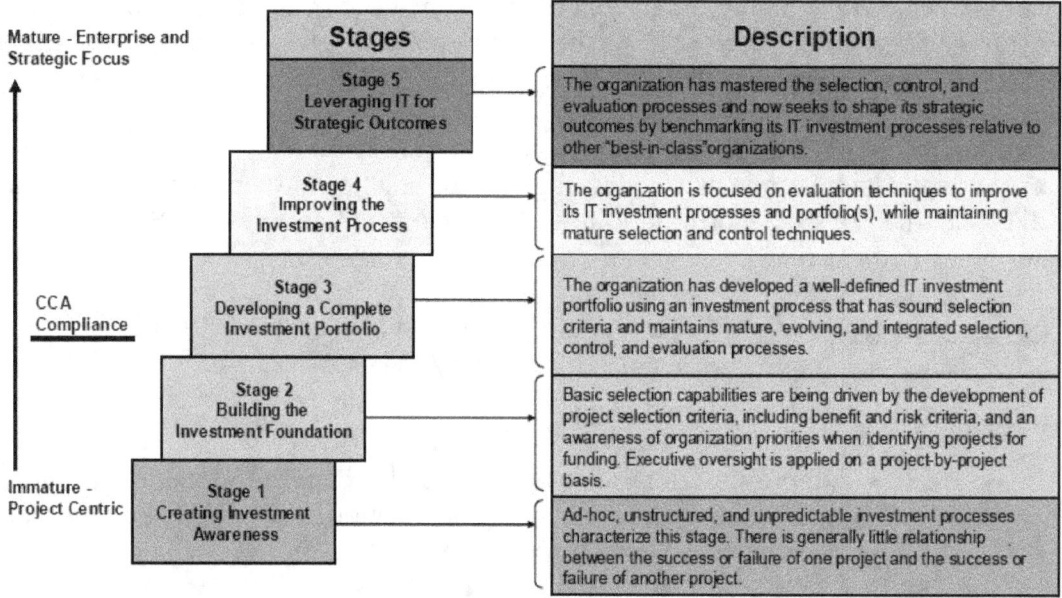

	Stages	Description
Mature - Enterprise and Strategic Focus	Stage 5 Leveraging IT for Strategic Outcomes	The organization has mastered the selection, control, and evaluation processes and now seeks to shape its strategic outcomes by benchmarking its IT investment processes relative to other "best-in-class" organizations.
	Stage 4 Improving the Investment Process	The organization is focused on evaluation techniques to improve its IT investment processes and portfolio(s), while maintaining mature selection and control techniques.
CCA Compliance	Stage 3 Developing a Complete Investment Portfolio	The organization has developed a well-defined IT investment portfolio using an investment process that has sound selection criteria and maintains mature, evolving, and integrated selection, control, and evaluation processes.
	Stage 2 Building the Investment Foundation	Basic selection capabilities are being driven by the development of project selection criteria, including benefit and risk criteria, and an awareness of organization priorities when identifying projects for funding. Executive oversight is applied on a project-by-project basis.
Immature - Project Centric	Stage 1 Creating Investment Awareness	Ad-hoc, unstructured, and unpredictable investment processes characterize this stage. There is generally little relationship between the success or failure of one project and the success or failure of another project.

FY10 – FY 15 Objectives

- Process all credit card purchases in compliance with NTSB regulations and timelines
- Process all PRs in compliance with NTSB regulations and timelines
- Phased approach to achieve CPIC process maturity during FY10 – FY15
    - 90% of IT investments will be within 10% of the goals established in the cost, schedule, and performance baseline **(FY11)**
    - Synchronize Capital Planning activities with those of Enterprise Architecture and Information Security
    - 95% of IT investments will be reviewed and approved through the CPIC process
    - 95% of IT investments will be within 10% of the goals established in the cost, schedule, and performance baseline **(FY12)**
- Achieve Level 3 of the GAO ITIM Maturity Model *(FY12)*
- Achieve Level 4 of the GAO ITIM Maturity Model *(FY14)*

Stretch Objective(s)

- Reach GAO ITIM Maturity Model benchmarks ahead of schedule

Focus Area 5: IT Infrastructure

The Safety Board acknowledges that standardizing operational capabilities, such as through standard desktop, laptop and server configurations and secure wireless communications, is an essential component for attaining the desired level of maturity in the focus area of IT Infrastructure. A mature IT Infrastructure serves as a platform for continued standardization, and provides the capability to measure overall service level improvement. In an effort to increase the maturity level of the Safety Board's IT Infrastructure, the Office of the Chief Information Officer will continue to move toward infrastructure lifecycle planning, by factoring replacement costs into annual budgets as a continuing cost of doing business. The OCIO will also adopt the Information Technology Infrastructure Library (ITIL) framework to provide improved service quality to the Safety Board's customers.

Long Term Strategic Goal

The goal of this focus area is to provide enhanced enterprise operations capabilities — improving the quality, accessibility, and sharing of data between NTSB and its customers. The overall goal of this focus area is to provide improved levels of service and security within a cost-effective, value-added operational structure.

Operations Performance Analysis will be applied to activities in this area. The analysis will identify opportunities for improvement. This approach will allow the Safety Board to provide continuous improvement in operations performance.

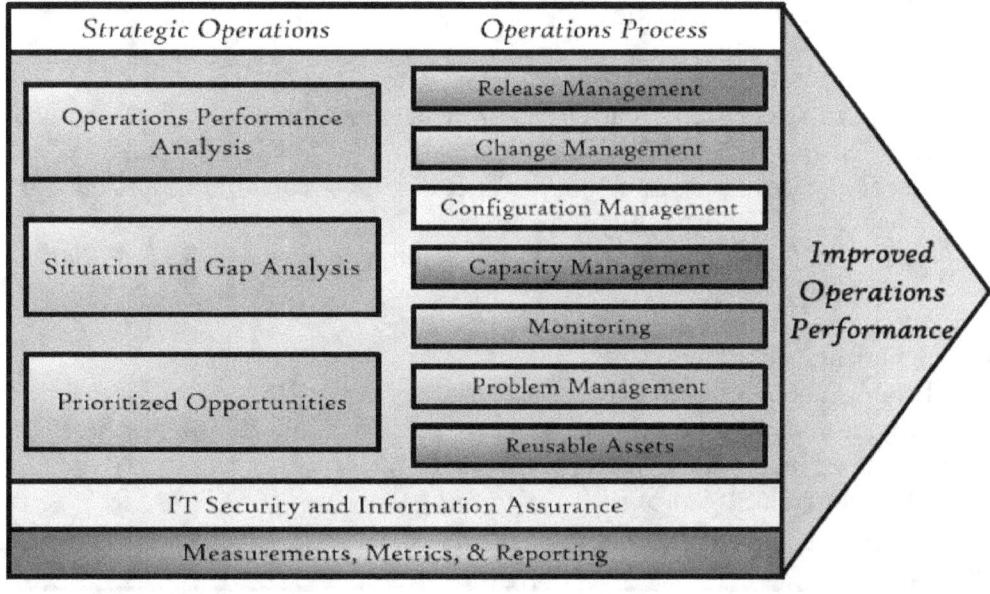

* ITIL was produced by the UK Office of Government Commerce.

Process Maturity Model/Performance Measure

The Safety Board will use the **Information Technology Infrastructure Library (ITIL)** to track progress in this strategic area and to provide quality IT service in the face of budgetary constraints, skill shortages, system complexity, rapid change, current and future customer requirements and growing customer expectations.

FY10 – FY 15 Objectives

- Asset Management
  - Enhance IT Asset Management Program by fully utilizing COTS asset management solution

- Customer Service
  - Develop FAQ page for common incidents and services
  - Initiate phased approach to reach ITIL process maturity FY10 – FY15
    - Service Level Agreements (SLAs) in place and met for 95% of cases for 20 most common incident and service request
    - SLAs in place for 100% of incident and service requests
    - SLAs met 98% or more of the time, documented reasons for all cases where SLA is exceeded
    - Meet network SLA provisions

- Infrastructure Management:
  - Have standard configurations for laptops, desktops and servers
  - Implement FDCC across the Safety Board
  - Achieve state where IT equipment is operating at no more than 2 release behind on operating system software
  - Implement fully operable development and test environments to support enhanced ISDLC activities

- Continuity of Operations (COOP)
  - Work with the Safety Board's senior management to prioritize IT resource requirements for COOP
  - Develop phased plan to upgrade NTSB IT COOP capabilities and deliver enhanced COOP capability to plan
  - Update and integrate OCIO COOP Plan into overall NTSB COOP Plan *(annual)*

- Telecommunications:
  - Establish network SLAs
  - Provide enterprise solution to support secure wireless communication
  - Ensure agency-wide IPv6 capability *(FY10)*
  - Meet network SLA provisions *(annual)*

Stretch Objective(s)

- Have ITIL compliant IT infrastructure environment by FY15

Focus Area 6: Information and Records Management

NTSB recognizes the importance of sound information and records management practices and has developed goals to drive improvements in support of the Information Management areas that include: Records Management, Privacy, Information Quality, Knowledge Management and the Freedom of Information Act.

Long Term Strategic Goal

The goal of Information and Records Management is to provide the information needed to make thoughtful decisions, to inform our stakeholders and provide appropriate public access to information, and to protect sensitive information from inappropriate release.

Information and Records Management must support the Safety Board's workforce in managing an ever-increasing volume of information and provide for the retention of institutional knowledge (Knowledge Management) despite a growing numbers of retirees from Federal service. Information and Records Management that follows mandatory standards is a keystone for ensuring an effective and responsible knowledge-sharing environment and provides assurance to E-Government customers that the Safety Board is serious about its role of steward of their information.

The Safety Board also recognizes the need to provide timely and accurate information to a broad customer base through an effective Freedom of Information Act (FOIA) program. As a result, the Safety Board has moved aggressively to bring its FOIA program into full compliance with the E-FOIA Act of 1996 and other Federal mandates.   Specific metrics have been set over the life of this strategic plan to ensure that compliance is achieved and maintained.

Process Maturity Model/Performance Measure

Compliance with the Safety Board's FOIA improvement plan and the Department of Justice annual review will serve as the primary performance measures for the FOIA portion this strategic focus area. The periodic evaluation of FOIA programs across government, and NTSB's relative ranking in that evaluation, by the National Security Archive will serve as a secondary measure of the Safety Board's FOIA program. Compliance with NARA guidelines will serve as the performance measure for the Records Management portion of this strategic focus area.

FY10 –FY 15 Objectives

- Review the Safety Board's FOIA Improvement Plan and adjust as required
- Complete NTSB Electronic Record Schedule
- Meet the E-Government Scorecard requirements for "Maintaining Green":

- Demonstrated for 90% of applicable systems a Privacy Impact Assessment has been conducted and publicly posted; and
- Demonstrated for 90% of systems with personally identifiable information a system of records notice has been developed and published
- Complete Action items in FOIA Plan
- Gain NARA approval of NTSB Electronic Record Schedule
- Ensure compliance with Federal laws relating to Records Management, Privacy, Information/Data Quality, and FOIA *(annual)*
- Maintain backlog of FOIA requests of 50 at fewer cases for simple and complex requests *(annual FY10 and later)*
- Conduct FOIA training events to increase the visibility of the Safety Board's FOIA program *(periodic)*

Stretch Objective(s)

- Achieve rating of "E-Star Agency" in FOIA by The National Security Archive.

Focus Area 7: IT Workforce Management

A well-trained, experienced workforce is vital to providing excellence in IT services. Key focus areas include staffing, IT skills and competencies, role-based training, and succession planning. IT workforce management will leverage the Safety Board's Strategic Human Capital Plan (http://www.ntsb.gov/Abt_NTSB/Plans/Strategic_Human_Capital_Plan.pdf) and OPM's Workforce Planning Model to leverage the capabilities of this critical resource.

Long Term Strategic Goal

The goal of this focus area is to ensure the availability of IT human capital capable of meeting IT goals and NTSB mission challenges. This focus area includes:
- Improvement of IT workforce identification, assessment and reporting capabilities
- Ensuring that robust IT professional development programs are available; and
- Strengthening and leveraging IT project management skills;

Success in this area must also take into account changes to business processes, workloads and required skill sets that will result from implementation of enterprise initiatives, modernization blueprints and E-Government initiatives. As mentioned earlier the Safety Board has adopted OPM's Workforce Planning Model to ensure that IT human capital resources meet Safety Board mission requirements.

Process Model/Performance Measure

OPM Workforce Planning Model

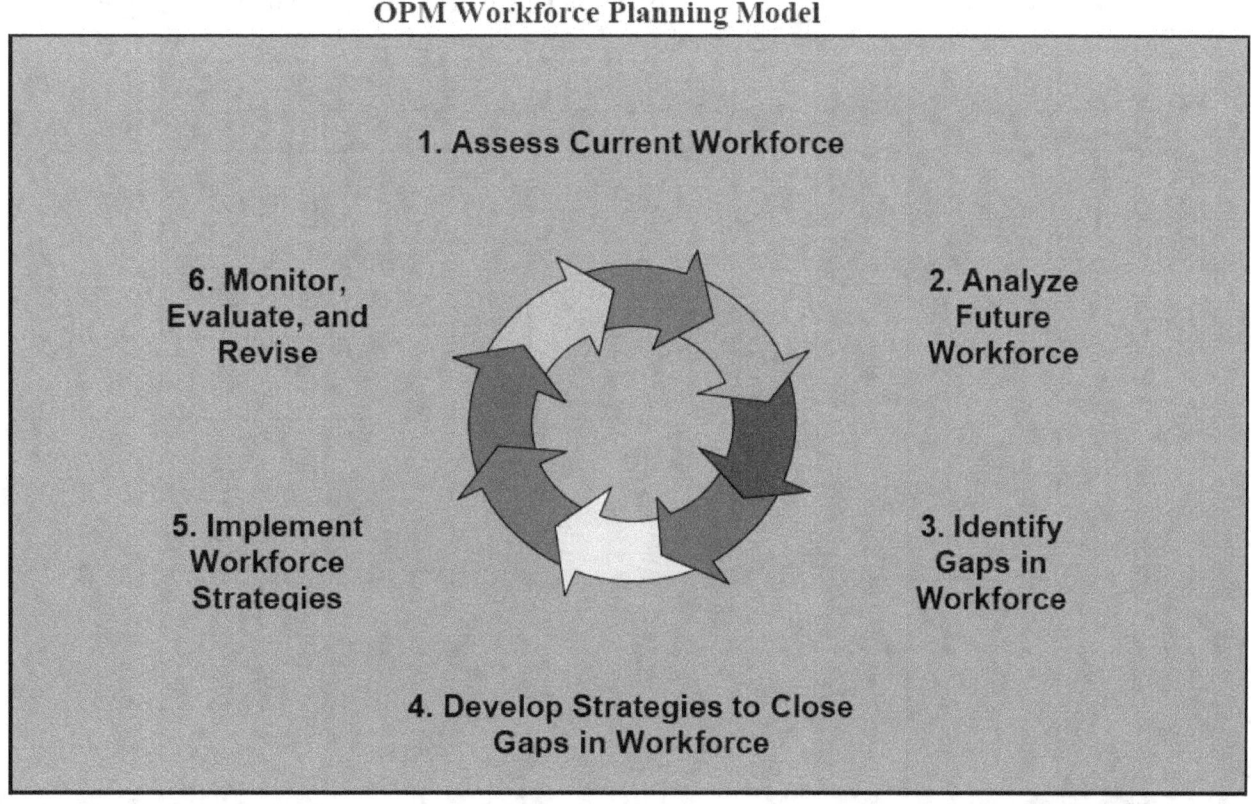

The Office of the Chief Information Officer also embraces the Safety Board's eight key human capital strategic objectives:

1) Enhance the recruitment process for critical occupations to attract well-qualified applicants

2) Develop an NTSB Strategic Training Plan and ensure the workforce has access to continuing training opportunities

3) Provide for the continued recruitment and retention of a highly skilled diverse workforce

4) Raise level of awareness of supervisory and management officials regarding leadership and management as perceived by the workforce

5) Strengthen the Performance Management System to align with organizational goals and objectives

6) Outline strategies for succession planning

7) Develop an NTSB Strategic Human Capital Plan that aligns with the NTSB Strategic Plan

8) Establish a project plan to monitor and evaluate the execution of human capital strategic objectives

FY10 –FY 15 Outcome Goals

- Refine and integrate baseline IT Human Capital and Training Plans with emerging agency-wide Human Capital and Training Plans *(annual)*
- Evaluate staff developmental progress against Human Capital and Training Plans *(annual)*

Stretch Goals

- No current stretch goal(s) for this focus area.

The National Transportation Safety Board's IT Strategic Plan provides a strategic framework for the coordinated development, implementation, operation, and integration of information technology within the Board.   The Safety Board's IT Strategy will enhance the efficiency and effectiveness of the organization as well as the support the successful delivery of Mission results.

Additionally, this document provides an organizational framework for the continued development of an architecture that can support more levels and types of electronic interactions. It outlines the Safety Board's IT Strategic Principles, establishes specific IT Strategic Goals with corresponding Focus Areas, and directs IT resources to utilize Maturity Models to measure performance. The Safety Board will strive for these collective approaches to improve performance, reduce inefficiency and duplication, and provide the support needed to achieve our important Mission.

The Safety Board will continue the migration of its IT portfolio toward integrated, agency-wide business processes and technologies to maximize the innovative and effective use of technology. Through leadership in customer service, strategic planning, intelligent management of IT resources and investments, and continual improvements in securing our IT environment, the Office of the CIO will provide high-speed reliable services that meet customer expectations and create savings.

> *As a key component in achieving the Safety Board's Mission, the Office of the Chief Information Officer will provide a viable means for ensuring that the Board receives the best value for its precious resources.*

APPENDIX – A
IT FOCUS AREA OUTCOME AND SUPPORTING OUTPUT\ACTIVITY MEASURES

The National Transportation Safety Board and the Office of the Chief Information Officer have a multi-layered performance management system that tracks outcomes[1], outputs[2] and activities[3]. A summary of performance for each IT focus area for the period FY2007 – FY2009 is provided on the following pages to demonstrate performance under the original IT Strategic Plan and to set expectations for FY2010 – FY2015.

Enterprise Architecture

The desired outcome for Enterprise Architecture (EA) was the establishment of an Enterprise Architecture Program at NTSB. That outcome was achieved through the following outputs and activities:
- Hired Enterprise Architect,
- Synchronized EA activities with those of Information Security, Capital Planning, Strategic Planning, Program Management Office,
- Completed initial TRM, BRM, SRM and PRM models,
- Initiated Business Process Modeling,
- Developed and Implemented a Configuration Management Process, and
- Published Enterprise Architecture Transition Roadmap.

For FY2010 – FY2015 the desired outcome of the Enterprise Architecture Program is to build upon the current foundation and to effectively use EA to make sound business and technology decisions.

IT Security

The desired outcome for IT Security was to remove the material weakness with respect to Federal Information Security Management Act (FISMA) compliance and to establish an effective FISMA compliant IT Security Program. That outcome was achieved through the following outputs and activities:
- Removal of Material Weakness with Respect to FISMA compliance,
- Addressed 100% of outstanding Department of Transportation's Office of Inspector General recommendations, and closed or made progress against General Accountability Office (GAO) recommendations,

---

[1] For the purposes of this appendix, an outcome is defined as a significant change in the state of a particular IT focus area, and includes events such as the establishment of a program, moving a program from an unacceptable state of performance to an acceptable state of performance or improving the overall maturity of the process.

[2] For the purpose of this appendix an output is defined a deliverable that supports the accomplishment of an outcome.

[3] For the purpose of this appendix an activity, event or series of events that support the accomplishment of an outcome.

- Completed Certification and Accreditation (C&A) for 66.67% of NTSB systems,
- Encrypted 100% of Safety Board's Mobile Computing Assets provided to headquarters and field office personnel,
- Provided annual IT Security Awareness training for 100% of individuals with NTSB network accounts,
- Provided annual Privacy training for 100% of individuals with NTSB network accounts,
- Provided additional specialized role based IT Security and Privacy training as appropriate,
- Enhanced existing policy, procedure and guidance capability to ensure the foundation of the NTSB IT security program,
- Enhanced security controls and procedures for the protection of privacy data and other sensitive data for mobile computing devices, internal databases and applications, and remote access solutions, and
- Integrated IT Security into NTSB projects via the Information Systems Development Life Cycle (ISDLC).

For FY2010 – FY2015 the desired outcome of the IT Security Program is to maintain FISMA compliance, maintain or improve annual FISMA Report scores and adapt to anticipated changes in the Government's approach to IT Security.

E-Government

The desired outcomes for E-Government were the establishment of enhanced structure for IT projects, deploy new products and update aging applications, and make greater use of E-Government initiatives. These outcomes were achieved through the following outputs and activities:
- Initiated standard Project Management training in partnership with NTSB's Training Center,
- Deployed new COTS-based Help Desk system,
- Established Web Guild,
- Implemented RSS Feeds,
- Deployed FOIAExpress system,
- Ascertained Section 508 Compliance,
- Upgraded DMS architecture,
- Updated Information System Development Life Cycle to support:
    - Enterprise Architecture,
    - IT Security,
    - Capability Maturity Model Integration (CMMI) Level II,
    - Data Privacy,
- Conducted NTSB web standards compliance reviews on NTSB web sites,
- Deployed e-ADMS in production environment,
- Enhanced DMS functionality, and
- Enhanced Safety Board's use of regulations.gov.

For FY2010 – FY2015 the desired outcomes of E-Government are to develop, maintain, and facilitate a sound and integrated web-related information technology architecture for the Safety Board by improving the quality of the Intranet and Internet web sites, implement solutions that support the Open Government Initiative, continue to leverage E-Gov/center of excellence solutions as appropriate and to further develop IT Project Management skill sets within the E-Government team.

IT Capital Planning and Investment Control (CPIC)

The desired outcome for IT Capital Planning and Investment Control (CPIC) was the establishment of a CPIC process at NTSB. That outcome was achieved through the following outputs and activities:
- Established basic business case template for IT Investments,
- Developed business case for IT Infrastructure refreshment,
- Developed IT CPIC procedures in accordance with Government best practices and aligned to GAO's ITIM Model,
- Provided CFO with three year budget forecasts for TechRep and OCIO support requirements, and
- Established and maintain OCIO budget control sheets to track expenditures in a timely manner.

For FY2010 – FY2015 the desired outcome of Capital and Investment Control (CPIC) is to continue to enhance and refine NTSB's CPIC process in line with accepted best practices.

IT Infrastructure

The desired outcome for IT Infrastructure was to improve the performance of the NTSB's IT infrastructure in the five key areas highlighted below. That outcome was achieved through the following outputs and activities:
- Asset Management
  - Installed LANDesk to support IT Asset Management program,
  - Installed a COTS based software solution to manage NTSB accountable property,
- Customer Service
  - Installed Heat system to provide enterprise support for incident, service and change management processes within OCIO and expanded the service to the Office of Administration,
- Infrastructure Management:
  - Encrypted 100% of mobile devices in compliance with OMB-06-16,
  - Evaluated requirements to create fully operable development and test environments to support enhanced ISDLC activities,
- Continuity of Operations (COOP)
  - Evaluated COOP capabilities at Ashburn facility,

o   Identify and acquired additional resource needs to provide email and blackberry connectivity should the Safety Board's Headquarters site become inoperable,
- Telecommunications:
  o   Upgraded network capacity to field and headquarters locations,
  o   Implemented tools to monitor and enhance network utilization,
  o   Conducted small scale pilot efforts to support wireless communication, and
  o   Met June 30, 2008 IPv6 requirements.

For FY2010 – FY2015 the desired outcome of IT Infrastructure is to continue to improve customer service, work against a standard tech refresh cycle, improve communications and COOP capabilities and effectively manage IT assets..

Information and Records Management

The desired outcome for Information and Records Management was to improve the performance of the NTSB's FOIA Program. That outcome was achieved through the following outputs and activities:
- Initiated use of FOIAExpress system in support of the Safety Board's FOIA program,
- Set and published rates and exclusions for FOIA charges,
- Executed all FY07 - FY09 milestones in the Safety Board's FOIA Improvement Plan designed to improve the overall effectiveness and efficiency of the FOIA program as well as customer service,
- Updated NTSB Internet FOIA site to comply with requirements of E-FOIA Act of 1996,
- Eliminated FOIA backlog,
- Began Posting Public Docket material for all modes on NTSB's website on June 1, 2009, and
- Completed FOIA training for non-modal offices.

For FY2010 – FY2015 the desired outcomes of Information and Records Management is to monitor performance of the FOIA program, make modifications to the program based upon additional requirements and to update the NTSB's Record Schedules.

IT Workforce Management

The desired outcomes for IT Workforce Management were to develop a baseline of IT Workforce skills and competencies, emphasize the importance of human capital and integrate IT Workforce Management into the NTSB's Human Capital Planning process. These outcomes were achieved through the following outputs and activities:

- Conducted Workforce Skills and Competency Assessments,
- Developed baseline IT Human Capital and Training Plans,

- Completed IDPs for 100% of OCIO Staff,
- Integrated a "Professional Development" rating element into performance plans for supervisors, managers and employees, and
- Integrated OPM's Workforce Planning Model and NTSB's eight key human capital objectives into the focus area

For FY2010 – FY2015 the desired outcome of IT Workforce Management is to continue to map to current OPM and NTSB-wide Human Capital and Training Plans.